Giselle

GISELLE
A Role for a Lifetime

with the text of the ballet scenario
adapted from Théophile Gautier

by VIOLETTE VERDY

with Ann Sperber

Illustrated by
Marcia Brown

MARCEL DEKKER, INC.

NEW YORK and BASEL

Library of Congress Cataloging in Publication Data

Verdy, Violette, 1933-
   Giselle: a role for a lifetime.

  (The Dance Program; v.5)
  1. Giselle (Ballet) 2. Adam, Adolphe Charles,
1803-1856. Giselle. I. Sperber, Ann, joint
author. II. Gautier, Théophile, 1811-1872.
Giselle. III. Brown, Marcia. IV. Title.
V. Series.
GV1790.G5V47   792.8'4   77-10789
ISBN 0–8247–6525–7

MARCEL DEKKER, INC.
270 Madison Avenue, New York, New York 10016

Current printing (last digit)
10 9 8 7 6 5 4 3 2 1

PRINTED IN THE UNITED STATES OF AMERICA

To the dancers who have made *Giselle* live

Foreword

The ballet of *Giselle* was first performed in Paris, in 1841. The scenario, by the poet Théophile Gautier and the librettist Jules de Saint-Georges, was based on a folk tradition mentioned in the writings of the German poet, H. Heine. The ballet, with choreography by Coralli and music by Adolphe Adam, was an instant success. Shortly after the première, Gautier acknowledged his debt to Heine in a charming open letter published in *La Presse*. In a later article, Gautier described *Giselle* in full detail for the benefit of the reading public. The text presented here is a free translation of the main body of the article, wherein Gautier tells the story of the ballet. For purposes of narrative, several literary allusions have been elided. In that same spirit and in keeping with present production practices, the narrative ends not with the reappearance of Bathilde, included in the original scenario, but the final farewell of Giselle. The complete French text, with its contemporary references to Carlotta Grisi, Fanny Elssler, and *Giselle's* authors, may be found in Gautier's *Les Beautés de L'Opéra*, a collection of writings covering twenty-five years of theater life in Paris.

A Role for a Lifetime

I never prepared anything in my whole life as much as I did Giselle.
It's a role that grows with you, opening up new aspects at every
stage of your career and your own personal development. It's also
a role that poses enormous technical and dramatic challenges; how
you rise to these challenges at different stages of your life adds of
course to the fascination of Giselle, both for the dancer and the
audience.

I have danced most of the classic heroines, including the Swan
Queen and the Sleeping Beauty. But Giselle is special: it gives you

1

the chance literally to give all of yourself and by the same token to discover how much you have to offer—in terms of the disappointments as well as the successes. Giselle gives you a chance to explore all your capacities; you have to be a complete dancer and a complete person.

I first learned the role of Giselle in Paris with the Russian emigré dancer and ballet master Victor Gsovsky. I remember how we worked every morning: first, a class; then he would teach me the great roles—Coppelia, Beauty, the Swan Queen, all the classics. Giselle he started teaching to me very slowly, deliberately, from start to finish. He had worked on it a great deal with Markova, having been ballet master for a time with the Markova-Dolin company, so that he was able to explain everything—all the different roles, their techniques, their attitudes, their style—all of this he was able to impart to me. In turn, I came to understand the story and quite literally fall in love with it.

For me, this was a very rich, complete world. I was very young and had not seen that many Giselles; its performances were confined to the Opéra, where it was staged only occasionally. So it was first through Gsovsky that I learned not only about Giselle but about the ballet itself, the characters, their reactions—through a single person, through *all* of him as the great ballet master that he was.

After Gsovsky, I got to really performing the role with the Marie Rambert company. With her background in modern dance, ballet, and eurythmics, she had quite another view of Giselle—a dramatic, impulsive, free sort of approach. Her concept, the Giselle that she advised, was a highly impetuous, passionate, lyrical-dramatic heroine; not the confined, Romantic, studied Giselle of the lithographs. It was an approach more related to Isadora Duncan than to Pavlova, certainly, but valuable in its way, capable of transforming her own ballerinas, who were admittedly not great technicians, into *apparently* great dancers, carrying the audience along with the conviction of their portrayal.

Years later when I restudied the role for my first Giselle in America, I finally came to Dimitri Romanoff, the Ballet Master of Ballet Theatre and one of the best people working today; he came out of the Russian tradition and also worked with Fokine in Ballet Theatre's early days.

Dimitri is among those trained by the great Russian emigrés—dancers like Bolm and Mordkin, who had worked with Pavlova, who were formed in Russia, who were carrying on the tradition of Trefilova, Pavlova, the Diaghilev dancers who left before the Revolution as well as those who got out shortly afterward.

I watched Romanoff at work for days on end—the company was the Boston Ballet, my Albrecht Edward Villella—and I learned even more details than I had picked up from Gsovsky. In fact, I decided, then and there, that working with Romanoff would be worth forgetting practically everything I had learned previously, and starting from scratch. And I'm very happy that I did. Because I cannot work on Giselle without going right back to the very beginning each time I dance it. I have to start out again—completely. To try to recapture her youth, her spirit, her freshness, her innocence, her belief, her aspiration, her joy; I am *forced*, with the character that I represent, to begin anew.

Over the past years, I have managed to see many of the good and some of the great Giselles and here I must think in particular of those I saw first in Paris, beginning with Yvette Chauviré—a woman of great heart and the first Giselle I could really observe. She was right in the tradition; she had worked with Lifar but more importantly, with Boris Kniasev who had been close to Spessivtzeva for so many years.

Hers was a Giselle portrayed right from the heart, with real feeling. You were *so* conscious of her love for the dance and her love for Albrecht that the end, when it came, was almost unbearable.

Yvette was also one of the first French ballerinas to revive another tradition — that of the dedicated dancer who is almost a nun, wedded to her vocation. She had an unequaled sense of costume and presentation. Not having the tallest, or the most slender, or the most perfectly proportioned body, she had to create those illusions with her art.

She was not, for example, a great jumper; but she knew how to give an impression of lightness in the second act. I remember how she told me of watching through a keyhole at the Paris Opéra, observing Spessivtzeva practicing alone for hours on end, and learning. She had seen the other great ballerinas — in a somewhat more orthodox fashion, *bien entendu*, and so had gradually absorbed the style of that second act; its Romantic repose, its quiet, its suggestion of other worlds. What she could not achieve, therefore, with pure action — what Makarova might do today, for instance, with that fantastic jumping and covering of space — Yvette did with an impression, and also with poses that were absolutely breath-catching, they were so beautiful.

Vyroubova, I remember, was an extraordinarily interesting Giselle, projecting a strongly Romantic feeling. I particularly liked her second act, where the arms and the general look of her shoulders, neck, and head were quite beautiful in an old-fashioned way. Hightower was not beautiful in the accepted sense but oh, how she could dance! She was so strong, yet so touching, the sense of betrayal very intense. Markova was of course unforgettable: that little figure, so perfect for the part, so right from beginning to end. Her strange, waif-like quality in the first act and her looks in the second act; and the dancing — those marvelous little feet, the lightness of her, the general quality of her style and feeling.

Ulanova, however, was unique, the only one of that generation who to my recollection could be judged by the same standard as Markova.

I first saw Ulanova in the late fifties and will never forget the strongly personal impression she made on me. She wasn't pretending to look fragile—which she was not—or strange, or unusual. She was doing it with her own truth, and with such conviction; a dancer of the head as well as heart. Yet though you could see a good head at work there, somehow the intellect didn't get in the way. The reading was completely integrated into what she was herself. To paraphrase Goethe a little, it was poetry—danced poetry—and it was truth.

At the time, in what I can only call my first rapture, I noted my impressions and would like to share at least a few of them.

"The Markova interpretation," I wrote at the time, "is the yard-stick by which we set the standards even now for all other dancers..."

...her lightness; the poetic effacement of effort, even at times of the steps themselves; the essential poetic fragility of the apparition; a supernatural creature, a shadow, a phantom. But—but—a being without heart, without feelings (not necessarily human feelings; she is after all an elusive spirit); it is an interpretation in which the beauty of the "vision" satisfies you in itself. She is simply a vision that dances divinely.

Ulanova is quite another matter. To begin with, the schooling is entirely different; the Soviets have not undergone the influence of Isadora Duncan or the latter's influence on Fokine, influencing in turn the purely classic dance. Therefore, the form is always complete, generous, full; the arabesque for example is always high, never "à la Fokine." This is an important point, since it is the form that impresses you at the outset.

What Ulanova possesses—an essential quality, in my opinion, univer-sal in interpretive dance, and what one rediscovers constantly in all the greatest dancers—is heroism. This heroism—call it grandeur, breadth, profundity, the ultimate dimension of technique and interpretation—is the hallmark of any great interpretation become complete and comprehensible and simple—accessible to the elite as well as to "the greatest number."

Then, there is the essential quality, which so many dancers forget in Giselle, and which is love: such a powerful determinant in the first act—for if Giselle is not truly mad with love, how can one be transported and interested, and above all, moved?

Moreover, if a dancer forgets, in the realistic first act, that Giselle has found a great love, how can she successfully convey that feeling with clarity (and with even greater strength and profundity) amid the paradoxical abstractions of the second act?

One above all, in my opinion, understands this—Ulanova.

Her interpretation of the second act is sublime. Absolutely transcendent. Danced in the most beautiful and large, yet most intimate manner imaginable, but above all expressing constantly, throughout the act, the redeeming love of Giselle for Albrecht, her sacrifice to save him, preserving all the while an other-worldly quality, never quite "human"....

And finally, a dancer who as Giselle is not ashamed to have this admirable technique, who plays the part devoid of hyprocritical weakness; who enters the scene without saying, in effect, "Excuse me for coming to dance," but on the contrary—"I have something important to tell you—voilà!" And everyone understands and is gripped.

This is definitively the great danseuse of our epoch. If you see her first act, it is unimaginable in its innocence, beauty, simplicity; she is 15 years old. One need not believe, one is transported.

And how she dances! The most sensitive and delicate feet; the music is Ulanova, as she is the music.

The example of the great interpreters is of course important to one's own work. You must literally fill yourself with the great examples of your time and your vision. And you must revel in the joys and the richnesses of the live performances. It's perfectly all right, even essential for a dancer who's going to work on a part to be completely entranced, fascinated, captivated—I might almost say concluded—by a great performance. But you cannot stop at that. If you're going to do it yourself, you must discover how. You cannot just borrow. This is where the teachers come in: they are the bearers of the tradition, with all its ramifications. They can evoke an atmosphere, a certain interpreter, even a number of inter-preters, to teach you the part.

Both elements, therefore—the great visual examples and the great teachers—are absolutely necessary.

But—and this is a big *but*—when the moment of truth comes for yourself, you can no more imitate those examples outright than you could slip into someone else's skin. You must go back to the *why* as well as the *how*. What did they go through, those performers, in order to do what you saw there on the stage? That gesture—what did they do to find it? That's where you go right back to the begin-ning and analyze—as I have said, start from scratch. *Bon*. You try the gesture, *feel* its content. Because the content has an emotion and an intention, and only by trying can you rediscover it for yourself. Does it seem right to you? If not, you must change the gesture and find out what *is* right for you, what it is that you want to say, to represent. For content cannot be imitated; it must be understood.

In spite of those moments of adoration, therefore, or even the occasional discouragement (*well, it's been done, why should anyone bother?*), the dancer must always come back to herself and the process of self-discovery; only in this way is it possible to build a role.

As I stated at the outset, my fascination with this ballet has been a lifelong love affair. What traditions cannot be related to it—the poetry and philosophy of the Romantics, the classic ballet, folk tales relating back to pagan times, even the dancing god-creators of ancient India; what cannot be caught up in its wilis' veil? It weaves an enchantment as subtle and all-embracing as the spell cast by Myrtha's wand of marsh flowers. I often think of the desolate areas of my native Brittany; heaths overgrown with broom and gorse and heather; swamps known as *La Lande*, where strange fumes rise in the early morning and fogs roll in from the sea. Young men in particular used to be warned against meandering late at night in La Lande, for fear of the will-o'-the-wisps, the little fairy lights that were supposed to set you dancing and drive you mad. And while we Bretons didn't quite make wilis of them, we did come up with a peculiarly Celtic sprite called a *Korrigane*, which incidentally also served as the theme of a ballet.

A word about the background of *Giselle*: We sometimes forget just how much the nature spirits—the wilis, viljas, ondines, roussalkas —fascinated the choreographers of nineteenth century Europe. Ondine, in *La Fille du Danube*, was a celebrated Taglioni role. *La Korrigane*, based on Breton nature themes, was mounted by the Opéra in the 1880's. Leafing further through the Opéra's annals, we also find a *Roussalka*, unrelated to the Dvořák opera of the same name, produced in 1911 and following closely the story line of Giselle: the betrayed village girl who, deceived by her noble lover, takes her life only to be resurrected in the second act as one of a band of nature spirits. In this case, however, the penitent lover was saved by the heroine's pleas; the Water Queen, unlike Myrtha, turned the young Count into an immortal and the lovers were united forever.

The creator of *La Roussalka*, by the way, was the ballet master Ivan Clustine of the Moscow Imperial Ballet, a considerable talent whose life and career were unfortunately cut short by war and revolution and who, along with Trefilova, was the teacher of my own first teacher, Madame Rosann.

8

There is so much more that one can say about *Giselle*, but it is better said in context. Let us therefore turn to the ballet itself, and to Monsieur Théophile Gautier, poet and critic *extraordinaire*, writing in *La Presse*, Paris, 1841.

*My dear Henri Heine, while leafing through your beautiful book,
de l'Allemagne, a few weeks ago, I came across a charming
passage (one has merely to open the volume at random). It
was the passage in which you speak of white-robed elves
whose hems are always damp, of water nymphs who leave
traces of their little satin feet on the ceiling of the nuptial
chamber, of wilis as pale as snow, those unpitying waltzers,
and of all the delicious apparitions that you have met in the
Hartz mountains and on the banks of the Ilse in the velvety
mist of German moonlight—and I said out loud, "What a
pretty ballet one might make of that!"*

In a rush of enthusiasm, I even took a large, lovely sheet of white paper and wrote at the top, in a superbly clear script: LES WILIS, ballet. Then I burst out laughing and threw the paper away without going any further, telling myself that it was certainly impossible to translate all of that into theatrical terms—that misty nocturnal poetry, that voluptuously sinister phantom world, all those effects of legend and ballad that have so little in common with our customs. That evening at the Opera, my head still full of your ideas, I met at the turning of a corridor the man of wit who, by adding so much of his own, knew how to infuse a ballet with all the fantasy and all the caprice of Le Diable Amoureux by Cazotte, the great poet who invented Hoffmann in the middle of the eighteenth century, according to the complete Encyclopedia. I told him the legend of the wilis. Three days later, the ballet of Giselle was finished and accepted. At the end of the week, Adolphe Adam had composed the music, the scenery was nearly completed, and rehearsals went into full swing. . . .

GISELLE

ACT I

*A*s the curtain rises you see, gilded by a warm shaft of sun-light, a steep bank of the Rhine in all the magnificence of its autumn dress. It is almost time for the vintage: the amber grapes are swell-ing beneath their leaves of russet and saffron. And in the depths of the valley flows the river Rhine.

A cottage, humble but charming, nestles in a corner, tucked away like a bird's nest among the vines and foliage. Opposite lies a small hut. And off in the distance, perched on the crest of a rock, shine the white pepperbox turrets of a lofty feudal retreat, one of

those frowning fortresses from whose heights the nobles, like so many vultures, would sweep down to prey on poor travelers.

From that castle—with gentler intentions by far—has come young Count Albrecht, a handsome lad of courtly bearing. From

the heights of his rock, the hawk has seen the dove fluttering in the plain. That dove is Giselle, a charming girl, the daughter of Berthe.

Now you might well imagine that knightly spurs, the arms of a nobleman, and a fine doublet of delicate fur would frighten away the modest Giselle. Even a simple girl knows that counts do not marry peasants—not even in the world of ballet. Albrecht knows it too. He has therefore come disguised as a young villager; only his courtly manners hint at his noble origin. He sends his squire Wilfred back to the castle while he himself remains behind in the hut facing Giselle's cottage, awaiting the greatest happiness a man can experience, especially if he is rich and powerful: the happiness of being loved for himself.

Daylight is breaking. The cottage door opens a little and Giselle darts forth, nimble and joyous as only the pure-hearted can be. Now what would a young girl think of first, when rising in the early morning, all in the red flush and fragrance of dawn? Would she take a basket and sickle and run off to the vineyard? Those who would say "yes" know but little of a maiden's heart.

No indeed! Giselle senses the presence of her love. He is there, alert and ready to dance. So at the risk of brushing the dew off a few flowers, she, too, is going to dance a little. That is only fair; she has not danced since yesterday—a whole long night spent between the cold sheets, without music, and with one's feet absolutely still—heavens! how much time has been lost!

For Giselle has one fault—at least that is what her mother calls it. She is mad about the dance; she dreams only of dances under green arbors, of endless waltzes, and of waltzers who never weary. Albrecht, known to Giselle only as Loys, is undoubtedly the perfect partner for her. He never interrupts the dancing with, "It is too hot, let us rest!" Loys is always ready to dance on and Giselle loves him with all the devotion of her warm heart. Indeed, what maiden would not be taken with a young gallant who never misses the beat, who never gets dizzy, and whose hands—unlike those of the village boys—are as white as if he had never done a day's work?

Yes, Loys is a fine dancer, but does he love as well as he dances? Young men today are so deceitful!

Flowers are more truthful. Here is a pretty daisy with a golden heart encircled by a wreath of silver, whose every petal, like a little tongue, knows how to spell a word in the book of the future—the future of lovers, of course.

Giselle picks the daisy. How her hand trembles as she plucks fearfully at the frail petals! *He loves me—a little, passionately, not*

at all! *Not at all!* answers the wretched flower and Giselle throws
it to the ground in despair. But Albrecht (or Loys, if you prefer)
retrieves the offending daisy and corrects the oracle: *He loves me*
—he loves me—he loves—loves—loves. A good-looking young
man can always make the flowers do his bidding.

Giselle is reassured. The cloud of sadness lifts, and laughter,
that pink flower of the soul, brightens her fresh features once again.

Joining her friends, she goes off to the vintage—much to the satisfaction of Mother Berthe.

So far all has gone well; but of all the good things in this life, the one most begrudged is happiness. People may forgive the rich for being rich, the powerful for being powerful, and the famous for being famous; but the happy are never forgiven.

A jealous eye is watching Giselle. Hilarion, a rough and mysterious gamekeeper straight out of an old German ballad, yearns for her with a love that borders on hatred, a love that consumes those twisted hearts who know they can never be loved in return. It is a love turned to bitterness.

Hilarion knows that Loys, far from being a peasant, is really a young lord of high and noble lineage, and that he is moreover betrothed to the fair Princess Bathilde. After breaking into Loys's hut through an open window, he has found the proof: the knightly sword, the spurs, and the emblazoned cloak.

With a word he can kill Giselle.

But see! The grapes have all been gathered. The villagers return
with brimming baskets, ready to celebrate. Giselle, crowned with
vine leaves and carried triumphantly aloft, is proclaimed the new

Queen of the Vintage. A rustic festival! What a splendid occasion for dancing. Everyone joins in, and above all Giselle, whose little feet cannot keep still.

"Wretched child," pleads Mother Berthe, "you will dance to
your death! And when you die, you will become a *wili*. You will go
to the midnight ball in a dress of moonlight, with bracelets of dew
clinging to your cold, white arms. You will draw the travelers into
a fatal round and then hurl them, all panting and streaming with
sweat, into the icy waters of the lake. You will become a vampire
of the dance!"

But Giselle answers these motherly chidings much as any daughter would when reminded by her mother that the hour is late: "I
am not weary—one more little *contredanse*—only one more!"

For Berthe's child is an incurable
dancer and not at all alarmed at
her mother's warnings.

What of it?
To dance on after death—
would that be so frightening?
Is it then such a pleasure to lie stiff and still
between six planks and two small boards?

Moreover, when a girl is pretty, young, and in love, how can
she believe in death?

Halloo! The shrill flourish of hunting horns echoes through the valley, followed by the barking of hounds straining at the huntsmen's leash. Horses prance and rear. It is the brilliant retinue of Princess Bathilde, out hunting with the Duke, her father.

Loys barely has time to slip away unnoticed.

The hunt has made the Princess weary and thirsty. She seeks a place to rest and taste the sweet milk and the fresh brown country

bread that princesses fancy. And, it happens, she is standing right in front of Giselle's cottage.

Mother Berthe appears with a great many curtsies, hand in hand with her daughter, who is ashamed to be caught thus unprepared for a visit by so great a lady. But the Princess seems so kind that one can almost forget how beautiful and noble she is, and how rich and powerful.

After having served Bathilde, the little village girl approaches her furtively. With the curiosity of a little cat, she stretches her hand toward the Princess and, as if by chance, strokes the rich, heavy fabric of her gown.

Bathilde, who has noticed the ruse, laughs with all the good humor of a great lady and places a long, finely wrought necklace of gold about Giselle's neck. Then she kisses the pretty peasant girl. Poor Giselle, flushed with pleasure and embarrassment, does not suspect that the proud Princess, swathed in velvet and jewels, is her rival; but it is so. The fatal truth is about to be disclosed in all its terrible light. For here comes that troublemaker, Hilarion.

May the devil take him, in his buckskin boots, his wolfskin cap, and his green jerkin!

He fetches Count Albrecht's cloak, spurs, and sword; Loys, returning all too soon, finds himself unmasked before Bathilde and the nobles.

Alas, sweet Giselle, your love was not what he seemed. A deadly chill seizes your heart, for great lords do not marry peasants. Besides, there stands Princess Bathilde, motionless in her surprise, and you cannot help but see her beauty.

A maiden's reason lies in her heart. When that heart is wounded, her reason falters.

Thus it is that Giselle lapses into madness—not the forehead-smiting frenzy of some disheveled heroine of melodrama, but a gentle madness, tender and sweet as Giselle herself. The music of the steps she danced with her beloved Loys, before he was Count Albrecht, comes back to her. She starts to dance, whirling faster and faster.

Suddenly, a flash of reason brings her back to the present. She tries to kill herself by falling on the sword brought by Hilarion. Loys quickly pushes the steely point aside, but it is too late. Giselle is wounded and will never recover. A few faltering steps, and she falls dead in her mother's arms, to the deep despair of Albrecht and even Hilarion, who now senses all the horror of his crime—for it is he who has killed Giselle.

Thus ends the first act.

Giselle has danced her way to death. But what of her repose after death? Who can forget Mother Berthe's sinister predictions and the legend of the wilis? The poor girl, alas, is not fated to sleep quietly in her grassy bed. To die at fifteen after going to scarcely a hundred dances and waltzing a mere two thousand waltzes! How do you expect that those charming little feet, more restless, more quivering than a bird's wings, will be still and not try to unwind the straight folds of the shroud, will not steal out into the moonlight to the glade where the rabbit polishes his whiskers with his paw, where the deer starts up, sniffing the air, his muzzle black and shining, there to frolic in the magic circle traced by the spirits of the night?

It is not life that one regrets leaving behind at fifteen—it is dancing and love, and not being able to leave the grave when one's beloved passes by, or inviting him for the next contredanse.

As for you, dear Albrecht, who never yet refused an invitation to dance, your future seems quite alarming, for it may well end with an icy bath in the waters of the lake or at the very least — double pneumonia.

ACT II

*T*he curtain rises on a mysterious forest, such as one sees in old prints. Tall trees with twisted trunks and tangled branches send their knotty roots plunging like thirsty snakes into the black, stagnant water. The wide leaves of the water lily and lotus unfold on the pond's surface. The tall grasses and ground plants mingle with the water reeds, whose velvety tips quiver in the night breeze.

A bluish mist bathes the spaces between the trees, creating fantastic shapes, the forms and movements of spectres. Are those the silvery trunks of aspens—or the pale shouds of ghosts? And does not the moon's sweet, sad, opal face, peeping through the tattered foliage, recall the transparent whiteness of a consumptive maiden?

The whole forest seems full of tears and sighs. Was it the dew or the rain that hung that pearl of moisture at the tip of that blade of grass? Is it indeed the wind that sobs in the reeds?

Who can tell?

Why is the velvet grass flattened only in certain spots? No human steps have ever ventured this far, nor is it from this bank that the herds of doe and roebuck descend to quench their thirst at the pool. This faint, sweet perfume is not that of wildflowers; the pink-centered bellflower and blue forget-me-not have no such fragrance.

Soon you shall come to the heart of this mystery.

In a corner overgrown by weeds and wildflowers stands a cross of stone, all new and white. A stray moonbeam reveals the name on the cross: GISELLE. It is there that Hilarion's victim lies buried in the cold earth, dead at fifteen.

But what can these bold hunters be doing in such a place? Instead of hare or deer, they will see only phantoms, against whom shot and gunpowder are unavailing.

This spot is haunted by evil, bold companions! Take your venison pie and your brandy flasks elsewhere. Listen! Midnight is striking—the uneasy hour when the living are gathered in and the dead go abroad. The will-o'-the-wisps, glittering butterflies of the night, begin fluttering about you. Scornful folk may laugh at will-o'-the-wisps and say they are caused by marsh gases, but you, worthy hunters, know that the glimmerings are souls in pain or evil spirits.

And you, brutish Hilarion, do not your shaky knees and the icy sweat that glues your hair to your temples, make you realize that you are close to Giselle's grave?

Brave as they are, the hunters take fright and flee. The spot is deserted, and the evening star, opening its silvery eyelids, pours a brighter light onto the clearing. Do you not see there, among the tall weeds, something like a trodden circle, showing the dancing place of the wilis? It is there that they celebrate their magic ball.

Look! The grass quivers, the heart of a four-o'clock unfolds, releasing a white vapor that soon condenses into the shape of a beautiful young girl, pale and cold as moonlight on snow. It is the Queen of the Wilis.

The tip of her wand traces cabalistic circles in the air as she summons her subjects from beyond the four winds. They are all women, these followers of Myrtha, as well they must be; men are too coarse, too stupid, too much in love with their own tough skins to die a romantic death. Their graves would never bear the epitaph:

He loved the dance too much;
it is that which killed him.

But see! Dancers from every country suddenly appear before the Queen: a fiery Andalusian, a melancholy German maiden, a baya-dere from India with golden rings in her nostrils, all who have lived, all who have died for and through the dance. They spring up from the earth, alight from the trees, come from every direction.

When all have assembled, the Queen proposes the admission of Giselle, a maiden who has just died.

Her dancing will do honor to their fantastic corps de ballet. As the others watch, the Queen points her magic wand, bound round with verbena, toward the tomb.

Suddenly, from amidst the undergrowth, a slender figure springs up, straight and white and stiff as though still in its coffin. It is Giselle, awakened from the heavy, dreamless slumber of the dead in their damp shrouds.

Raised from the dead and still very numb, she takes a few tottering steps. But soon the fresh night air and the silvery moonlight restore her high spirits. Joyfully, she takes possession of space once again. How freely she breathes, her chest rid at last of the stone's dead weight. What happiness—to be light and free again, to soar at will, alighting here or there like a capricious butterfly!

Humbly, she approaches the Queen of the Wilis and kneels
before her. A star is set upon her brow; two delicate little wings
unfold quivering from her shoulders. Two little wings and two
such feet—it is really too much!

The ceremony completed, the wilis prepare to teach their fantastic waltz to the young initiate. But their efforts are hardly needed; Giselle already knows it better than any of them.

Now, tardy travelers, take care! Do not pass the fatal clearing once midnight has struck, or your road may lead you to the bottom of the lake, down amid the muck and the reeds, with only the frogs for company.

At this very moment, a victim appears. The wretched Hilarion, haunted by remorse and led astray by a treacherous forest path, finds himself back where he started—the grave of Giselle.

The wilis grab at him. They push him on all sides, whirl him about, pass him down the line of dancers, from arm to arm, from hand to hand. His legs buckle under him—he struggles for breath; he begs brokenly for mercy.

No mercy! The waltzers of this world may be pitiless, but those of the next world are crueler still.

Hilarion is caught, released, then caught again. Every wili seeks a share in his destruction. And they are everywhere! Now there are ten—now twenty—now thirty of them! Into the water with you, Hilarion! You are weary, your feet are dragging. . . . Of what possible use is a tired dancer, except to be tossed into the lake?

At last, the ghostly little hands push the heavy, massive body over the edge of the bank. The water plashes, boils up; two or three circles spread, slowly dying, across the oily surface of the marsh.

Good night, Hilarion. Justice is done!

The leaves tremble; a hand parts the branches. Who dares approach this frightening spot at such an hour? It is Albrecht, maddened with grief, come to weep at Giselle's grave and to beg pardon of the beloved shade. For Albrecht did not wholly deceive Giselle, though he lied about his rank. His love was sincere and his words of love echoed the wishes of his heart.

Giselle, moved by Albrecht's tears, breathes a faint sigh—the sigh of a spirit. Albrecht whirls around to see two stars of azure twinkling in the foliage. They are her eyes—it is Giselle!

*Oh pity, matchless vision, do not vanish! Let me look once more
on that sweet face I thought to see again only in heaven.* And he
rushes forward with arms outstretched, but embraces only the reeds
and lianas.

A white vapor crosses the somber forest thicket. Once again, it
is Giselle. Hidden in a cluster of flowers, she plucks a few, touches
them to her lips, and throws the flowers with her kisses to her love.

But the wilis, ogresses of the waltz, have sensed the presence of a
fresh dancer. They rush in to claim their share of grisly pleasure.

Giselle clasps her hands in entreaty.

"Wicked ones!" she cries. "Leave me my Loys. Do not put him
to death. Let him live to enjoy the soft light of heaven, to remember me and weep upon my tomb. It is so sweet to feel a warm tear
penetrate beneath the earth, to feel it fall from a burning eye onto
one's cold heart."

"No, no, no! Let him dance and let him die!"

"Do not listen to them, my Loys. Cling to the cross on my grave.
Whatever you may see, whatever you may hear, do not leave it!

The cross is your refuge, it is your salvation. Its power can break
Myrtha's wand."

"True," says the Queen, with a commanding gesture. "My wand
loses its power before that cross. But you, Giselle, are subject to my
will. I order you to dance the most chaste and the most voluptuous
of dances, to look at him with your most tender glances, to smile
your most charming of deathly smiles. Albrecht will quit the cross
of his own accord."

Giselle, yielding despite herself to the powerful magic, obeys
with steps that are slow and languorous. Her furtive glance searches
the horizon . . . the night is passing. Surely the cock must crow
soon and day must break. If only Albrecht will cling to his sanctu-
ary, he will be saved. The unhappy shade tries to appear less beautiful, less seductive. Useless!

Now Myrtha forces Giselle to pour more energy into the dance.
Giselle must obey for she is a wili, after all. The intoxication of the
dance seizes her: she flies, she bounds, she whirls, and Loys, ob-
blivious to his fate, leaps after her and follows her steps, happy to
die in the arms of the beloved phantom.

The mad dance, brilliant and dizzying, seems to go on forever.
Albrecht pales. His breath comes in gasps. He is about to fall into
the treacherous waters when suddenly—

a far-off bell begins to strike the hour:

one, two, three, four o'clock.

A feeble bar of light takes shape in the clouds behind the hill; the
glimmer grows into a brightness. The wilis, frightened of the morning, scatter and reenter their hiding places in the hearts of the water
lilies, in the clefts of the rocks, and in the hollows of the trees.
Albrecht is saved.

Giselle sinks down onto the grass. The flowers enfold and close in over her, and her transparent body melts away like a vapor. Only her frail white hand still beckons in a last farewell to the love she must see no more. Then the hand, too, disappears. The earth has reclaimed its prey, never again to yield it up.

Albrecht tears frantically through the foliage, but he can see nothing. A single rose, plucked from the grave, is all that remains to Count Albrecht of the poor village girl. But it still breathes the chaste perfume of the soul of Giselle.

The curtain falls.

Dancing Giselle
A Guided Tour

For those undertaking the role of Giselle, perhaps the most important aspect to be developed is the contrast between the two acts—between the directness, the wonderful joyousness of the first act, and the Romantic lithograph effects of the second act.

In Act I, you dance with your whole body, with all the blood going. There are no inhibitions; the action is direct, open, and explicit. Giselle is young, she's a peasant girl, and she lives in the country. She is the epitome of what one hopes is freshness and innocence-but she is no aristocrat; she has good red blood in her veins and she breathes good country air. She is like some healthy, graceful young animal—therefore she jumps, she leaps, she employs free, full gestures. Only with Albrecht does Giselle show the inhibitions you expect in a Romantic heroine.

The second act is of course far different—blue-white moonlight, frozen gestures, the great adagio passages. How, then, does the dancer reconcile these two acts which are almost separate ballets? Here, both poet and choreographer provide a thread of continuity; it is the love of Giselle for Albrecht.

In the first act, the heroine is an innocent girl, in love for the first time, almost torn between that love and her love of the dance. The two forces are almost too much for one person, and therein lies the core of Giselle's tragedy. By the time we are into the second act, however, the love for Albrecht has become idealized. We see it mature until, selfless and strong, it conquers fear and ultimately, death itself.

Act I

The curtain goes up. Couples promenade. Harvesters stroll by, carrying their baskets. A little characterization may be thrown in during the opening measures: David Blair's American Ballet Theatre production, for instance, shows Hilarion buttering up *Maman Berthe*, bringing a freshly-caught rabbit, offering to draw water; less Gautier's sinister forester than an amiable *garçon* who's about to be outclassed.

Albrecht–Loys enters. He brushes off Wilfred's misgivings and, so to speak, takes up residence. To the young nobleman, Giselle is the embodiment of certain ideals—the freedom he cannot have, the carefree youth denied him, the innocence he cannot hope to possess. The Princess represents the call of duty. She's probably a very nice princess, but she's his father's choice and it's all very boring. But Giselle is his own discovery.

He knocks on the door of Giselle's cottage, then withdraws. The door opens, Giselle steps out, and begins dancing. The characterization is there right from the start, simply and naturally, as are all great moments in theater.

We know that Giselle is in love with Albrecht and we also know that she's in love with the dance. These are the two forces running parallel in her life. One seems ordinary enough: a young woman seeking a man to be happy with—though it will turn out to have no roots in reality, for Albrecht, though Giselle doesn't know it yet, is as unattainable for her as she is for him. The other force is a kind of ideal, the search for a way of being ideally happy, which is to dance. The classic dancer's conflict, therefore—the dance versus ordinary life—is already represented here, at the outset of Act I; and for Giselle, the only escape can be into death.

Within that context, the different ways of establishing the character are almost limitless. Ulanova projected a certain directness, purity, simplicity; the real emotions of a girl of fourteen or fifteen. Markova, on the other hand, with her delicate, waif-like quality, was just as innocent but somehow, strange; totally unlike the healthy girls around her—there was *something* different about that girl. With Markova, you really began to wonder: Who was Giselle's father? Was he perhaps a nobleman? Is that why Berthe is always fussing and worrying over her child? (Remember, no one ever mentions the father.) Is that why she is falling in love with a nobleman in disguise—blood calling to blood? You actually suspected something of the kind when you saw Markova.

With Chauviré, as I have said, you were above all conscious of the conflict between the two loves, preparing you for the tragedy to follow. What all great Giselles have conveyed, however, is that quality of innocence and above all, spontaneity. In that first act, she has to be *so* fresh, and *so* vulnerable; so much a young girl in the throes of first love. Because if it isn't for the first time, it has absolutely no interest for us—and there shouldn't be a mad scene, and there shouldn't be a broken heart, and there shouldn't be a death.

When I learned the opening, the scenario went something like this: Giselle hears the knock, opens the door, expects to find Albrecht. She doesn't see him, but the day is beautiful and she can dance. Very much *à la* Gautier. I have also seen this transformed into a scene where Giselle, not seeing Albrecht, turns the dancing into a search. But that shouldn't really take place during those first jumps. Those jumps are the spontaneous actions of a gazelle expressing herself as a gazelle. *Then* she starts looking for him.

At this point I remember Chauviré would do something extraordinary, making a charming monologue of the search. First she ran toward Albrecht's cottage, peeking around the corner to see if he was there; then, failing to find him, began to imagine what she would have done had he been there. She looked down at her dress, holding back the folds of the skirt: *Well, I would have curtsied to him—like this.* Then she seemed to say, *No, I wouldn't have done it like that. I would— oh, if only I could see him I would—I would curtsy to him like—this.* But that wouldn't seem right either. Here she drooped a little, disappointed—*Well anyway, he's not here*—turned to go, and found herself face to face with Albrecht.

In other versions, Giselle coquettishly imagines herself curtsying to him, stamps her foot in exasperation, and backs up, bumping right into him. This has a slightly more petulant quality—somewhat more soubrette in tone, with overtones of *La Fille Mal Gardée;* Lise meeting the boyfriend. The earlier Ballet Theatre production had something of that quality but however it is done, the opportunities for variety are right there from the start.

Giselle turns away and runs to the cottage door. He stops her, pleads; she comes back shyly. Here, two little scenes are most important to the characterization, and for what is to follow. First, Albrecht tries to kiss her hand, a most natural thing to do in his circle. But not in hers. She looks at him, withdraws, embarrassed, almost fearful. Nobody has ever kissed her hand, she didn't know it could be done; it seems so—private. Then, he puts her arm inside the bend of his arm. Again, she finds it's too close and too soon and too familiar. Very shyly, she disengages her arm from his and looks, questioningly: *Excuse me, what do you want?*

A little later, he invites her to sit down. In some versions Giselle spreads her skirts wide, to cover the bench. I find this a little obvious, too coquettish. Giselle should seat herself carefully—she is after all in the company of a suitor—but normally, just as she would always sit. She gets quite embarrassed, therefore, when he asks, *What about me? You haven't left me any room.* The idea of his sitting so close simply hasn't occurred to her. She looks at her skirt, tucks away enough to clear a corner of the bench, then turns from him with a certain amount of misgiving. She's right. For the minute he sits down, he moves closer—she moves away; he pushes further—she shifts again, until you can almost hear her clear her throat—*Ahem!* Finally she can't stand it, runs back to the cottage, and must again be reassured.

Remember, once Giselle spreads her skirts, the audience knows immediately that something's afoot. If she just sits normally, it gives her the opportunity to react—*Oh, he has no room* or *Oh dear, he's going to sit next to me;* it opens up a whole range of small but telling emotions which help further to define the character.

It was at this point that Chauviré did something very beautiful, which broke my heart the first time I saw it. Hers was a very shy Giselle, chary of being touched—which gave this moment its particular pathos.

Albrecht, you'll remember, raises his hand in oath: *I love you— I swear it.* And the village girl grabs his hand and lowers it, fearful of sacrilege. Here Chauviré stopped for just a small second and looked at the man's hand, with a sudden realization: *It's his hand that I'm holding now.* Then she became herself again—*You mustn't swear, it's not right*—looked over her shoulder toward the daisies—*Wait, I have something much better than swearing and all such things*—and went to gather them.

That whole scene, those little details, working up to the moment of, *Oh my God, I have his hand here for myself, just for a second*—that was Chauviré!

Giselle counts the petals of the daisy, something that a child of the country would do as naturally as saying grace in the morning—not as a matter of superstition but simply of being that close to nature. When the flower speaks, Giselle listens, knowing that nature does not lie.

Also, it's such a French thing to do, although as Gautier indicates, instead of "He loves me, he loves me not," we have more of a sliding scale: *Il m'aime, un peu, beaucoup, passionnément, pas du tout* (a little, a lot, passionately, not at all). I used to pluck each petal dutifully. Now I pluck the first time around, then count: one-two-three-four/one-two-three-four; yes/no/yes/no—knowing the game so well that after a time I know the outcome. Somehow I feel this is more in keeping with the character of Giselle—that in her youthful impatience to know, she doesn't even take time to pluck the flower entirely. Also, it is so much more refined and subtle to pluck the first—the second—the third, then just point and count, ending almost with a gasp: there's no more. And you drop the rest. In her heart of hearts, she knows already.

Of course *he* gets up quickly, runs to where she got the daisy, and comes up with another. In some productions he looks it over first, perhaps even removes a petal in full view of the audience—a sort of quick aside—just to be sure he'll have the right number. Then, very blatantly, presents it to Giselle: *You see? Yes!* He's already lying, of course, but he's so eager. Giselle, on the other hand, is almost conditioned for what's to come. Again, it is already written there: the heartbreak, the madness, and the death.

Hilarion intrudes on the lovers. In the age of the anti-hero he has changed from Gautier's bearded, brutal villain. David Blair's Act II opening even has him fashioning the cross for Giselle's grave. But Giselle is not in love with him and probably never was.

The dark hunter of German folklore and poetry—symbol of passion, eroticism, the darker side of love—was of course well known to the French Romantics. It is interesting to note that Weber's *Der Freischütz*, with recitatives by Berlioz, made its Opéra debut the same year as *Giselle*, the score already familiar to Parisians from other productions. The two works share the atmosphere of wooded glens, mystery and magic, princes and peasants, good versus evil; and Adam's robust horn passages for the royal hunting party echo the hunters' chorus in the earlier Weber work.

Hilarion, as Gautier reminds us, is a blood relation of the hunters of German balladry. He is primitive, perhaps, but not monstrous. One may think of him as a solitary man, more at home with wild pigs in the forest than with people, a man whose instincts reflect the darker aspects of nature and whose love, given provocation, might easily be transformed into hate. When Hilarion is provoked, therefore, he acts on pure instinct, without any resource or elevation of the spirit, blind to everything except his jealousy and his revenge. And Giselle, the rare flower that he had hoped to attain, will wither at his touch.

Giselle and Albrecht dance with their friends—at which point the Mother appears. It is very easy, and also very misleading, to portray Berthe as some kind of chicken-soup mama. Actually, she is a strong figure in her own right and it is encouraging to see some of the great companies—the Soviet troupes, the Royal Ballet, Ballet Theatre— restoring mime passages that had so long been cut from the Mother's part.

The original score seems to indicate that these passages were quite extensive. It is easy to see why: Aside from the fact that any extended characterization, well done, adds to the overall richness of the ballet, the Mother is an essential part of the atmosphere of over-protectiveness and even fear.

I have spoken of the mystery of Giselle's father; the Mother may just know something that we don't. Giselle may be fragile, even consumptive, with just a trace of aristocratic decadence about her, suggesting noble blood. The Mother, for her part—as a widow, a woman alone—has a well-developed sense of superstition that she has probably lived with much of her life. Like most country people, she loves these legends—but she also believes in them. The danger, she is convinced, is very strongly present in her child's makeup—in the fragility, the mad love of the dance; she sees it all too clearly.

There are many ways of conveying this. She may tell Giselle, *Oh, you have been dancing; your brow is wet,* and wipe her daughter's face with her apron. Giselle says, *Yes, I've been dancing with him,* to which she answers, *You know—I've told you that if you dance, you will die.* With that, she gathers the villagers around and goes into her monologue:

> *At night, when darkness comes, you see the crosses of the wilis. They come out of their graves, and they dance. And They'll get you, young man—and you, young man, and they'll dance with you and dance with you—until—you—die.*

With that, the whole second act is laid out before us, announced by the Mother in the form of an old superstition; apprehension preceding reality.

In some productions—the Royal Ballet of some years back, for example—there's even a reiteration of that warning, not once but several times, Berthe actually awakening those fears in her child, then reassuring her (*No, Dear, you're safe with Mother*). This, I feel, is not quite in keeping with Gautier though it raises an interesting point.

The image of the Mother, so loving and over-protective, also contains in the same sense the overwhelmingly destructive quality that a mother, alone with a daughter, can sometimes have. The Giselle–Berthe relationship, therefore, can be simply the practical woman watching over the inexperienced girl—or it can be the devouring power of the mother over a young daughter, expressed here in the form of superstition, instilling fear and a sense of fate in the child.

Berthe takes Giselle back into the house. Again, there are many ways of doing it. Some versions are quite elaborate, the Mother pulling Giselle along, Giselle in turn unaware that she's being hauled away, then looking distractedly at the source of the tugging — *Oh my God, it's Mother*. There may be a little debate (*But I want to stay with him/ No! This is enough!*). At which Giselle goes along dutifully with the Mother, turns around and escapes back to Albrecht, is caught up again by the Mother and finally consents, waving a last goodbye to her lover as Mother turns to the young man to say, *Get lost!*

There's a little opportunity for lightness here but again, one must avoid going into *La Fille Mal Gardée*. It must be consistent with the rest, part of the series of relationships — between Giselle and her mother, Giselle and Albrecht, Giselle and Hilarion — that make up the tapestry of *Giselle*, all the different little details, appearing and reappearing like interlaced *leitmotifs*, fragments in a lovely mosaic.

The royal party arrives, the wine is served. (Here I must think of Carla Fracci, bringing the wine to Bathilde and her father as they sit in front of the house. She serves them, sets down the jug, then wipes her hands on her skirt, just a little. And immediately you have a vision of those cool jugs, filled with rosé wine, left in a *cave* in the country and collecting the dew — all of that, conveyed in a single gesture.)

The longer Soviet versions have incidentally restored the secret exchanges between Bathilde and Giselle, both of them for the moment just two women, each in love, exchanging confidences as young girls will: *Are you engaged?/ Yes I am, what about you?/ Me too — he lives over there — look, this is the ring*. Lovely little things that are so nice and that make the climax, with its intrusion of reality, all the more heartrending.

The Princess and her father depart. Hilarion, alone on an empty stage, makes his discovery. The villagers return to celebrate the harvest, the lovers dance, only to be separated by the rejected suitor, bearing Albrecht's sword. The Count's secret is revealed and events move to their tragic conclusion. It's a long sequence and you have to ready yourself for it down to the smallest detail. The little earthenware jug, for instance, in which Giselle serves the wine—I make sure ahead of time that it will be waiting for me in the wings. Later, just before my solo, I may powder myself up a bit, not for the solo but for the mad scene—which comes later but then there won't be time—hoping that in the joy of dancing I won't look too pale. I also pin to my bodice the necklace that Bathilde has just given me so that it won't fly in my face when I do all those turns. The solo completed, I run into the wings and quickly unpin the necklace so that I can throw it at Bathilde's feet in the scene that is coming.

Then, while Giselle's friends are still dancing onstage, and prior to my reappearance with Albrecht, I partly unpin my coif, putting the flowers back in place to cover, so that the Mother can easily free my hair for the mad scene. I always check my haircut when I know I'm about to dance Giselle, so that there won't be too much thick hair, which is apt to become damp by the end of the first act, sticking to the face and the costume. I also try to keep my hair a proper length, away from the face, allowing the audience to see *me*; Giselle should look distracted, but not running about like some dishevelled doggy. Beyond these simple precautions, nothing more should be necessary; the scene should speak for itself, without tricks or effects.

Carla Fracci does something quite remarkable: Instead of undoing the whole coiffure, she loosens a single strand of hair—very black and, when set off against that white face of hers, very striking. The impression is like that of broken pottery; her little face, with that dark streak jagging across it like a broken line; a beautiful picture

68

with a break, a cut, a terrible flaw, that one disorderly streak of hair indicating the whole deranged mind.

But I can never think of that monologue without thinking of Gsovsky, teaching it on those mornings, years ago, in his Paris studio. In some ways it was the greatest portrayal of the Mad Scene I have ever known.

Victor was very tall, very thin. He smoked constantly and was a bit of an alcoholic—everyone knew that; he had those trembling hands and those strange eyes that were not clear. Consequently the Mad Scene became something fascinating to watch. Before my eyes, without lights or music, he turned into a lost being, almost retarded; there was just something indescribable there in the sense of loss and alienation. And another quality—something I couldn't find the word for until one critic used it in describing my own Mad Scene: cata- tonic—the stunned state besetting a person after a terrible shock. To me, this word seems altogether appropriate. Giselle does indeed enter another world, a kind of antechamber of death, in which the recognition of dying contrasts tragically with the episodes of remembering.

When, years later, I did the Mad Scene for Romanoff, he liked it so much that he advised me not to change anything. "Just do it."

"You know, it's all Gsovsky," I said.

"It's just wonderful," he answered. "I like it the way it is—keep it going."

But the dancer going through the Mad Scene should remember that the scene, as Gautier stresses, requires above all sweetness— a quality that will be touching rather than frightening, poetic rather than clinical. (The section, by the way, has been cut, the original score containing a brief, hymn-like passage denoting a fantasized wedding, somewhat à la Lucia di Lammermoor. In our day, the only traces of that passage may be brief, mimed references to a ring and a wedding veil, sometimes included in Soviet productions.)

Giselle takes the fallen sword, tries to kill herself. Albrecht succeeds in taking it from her but it is no use. She sinks lifeless in her mother's arms.

Lying immobile on the floor, surrounded by the mourners, you may feel somewhat wrung out yourself, after an hour of intense emotion. But your greatest test, as a dancer and an artist, is still ahead of you, in the act to come.

Act II

Giselle dies and is reborn. And we have gone from the bright sunshine of the vineyards to the moonlit realm of nineteenth century Romanticism: the escape into life-after-death, love idealized; the problems of the daytime world resolved, if only fleetingly, by the magic forces of the night; a conscious rejection of life and society that permeated the intellectual world of *Giselle*'s creators and would find its apotheosis a quarter century later in Act II of *Tristan*.

Giselle is now a shadow. The peasant girl has become the ideal Romantic woman—near-unattainable, very high *en pointe*, almost beyond reach, endowed with the extraordinary understanding of a supernatural being. Though she might never have been the wife, she has already become the mother—all the aspects, all the stages in a woman's life reflected in her relationship with Albrecht: she is at once the protective mother and the fiancée; she is the mistress, the woman, the mate.

The dancer portraying Giselle must therefore change her entire presentation. You must establish a "weeping willow" quality, all-enveloping, soft as mist. Your arms should be those of a creature of air and water; wet and heavy and soft. A walk becomes a glide, as though you were walking on clouds. The movements of the head, neck, arms, and feet are almost isolated, one from the other. Even the jumps take on a different quality; Giselle is no longer the exuberant village girl but a spirit, possessed and driven by an outside force. There must be no suggestion of the physical effort of dancing—which in turn, of course, demands far greater technical control. The legs that propel you through the air as a wili must be even stronger than in Act I. Passages calling for extreme lightness and fast footwork now alternate with the great, slow adagio sections danced both with and without Albrecht. After the emotional wear and tear of the first act, you must somehow find your way to the nerve-defying control that permits you to do these slow-motion variations.

For this act, as for Act I, Giselle wears a long mid-calf *tutu*, a costume I have worn in Balanchine ballets as well. It's wonderful to dance in, but it means changing the emphasis in the presentation of your body. The feet become *essentially* important: Because the full line of the leg up to the hip does not show up as it would in a short *tutu*, the footwork becomes the eloquent part of your legwork. You have to put your expression, so to speak, into your feet. I think Chauviré understood that better than anyone; it was one of her great trademarks, something absolutely related to the seventeenth century—that beautiful style of early ballet, with just the shoe appearing beneath the skirt, and perhaps the heel coming forward; she was so much a dancer in that tradition.

What you do with your feet, then, becomes a vital part of Giselle's vocabulary. You have to literally present them—they must be fleet, fast, very nicely pointed, caressing; you must work with them just as you would with your hands.

The costume itself is of great importance. For my *tutu*, I use a nylon material with just the slightest suggestion of a sheen to it—I call it "snail's spit"—and a very few sequins, scattered at wide intervals. The top layer is of wedding veil, a delicate and billowy silk net that settles very, very slowly and softly after each jump.

The overall impression is shimmery though not shiny—a moonglow effect, if you will. Different things can be done with the wings: they can be bigger or smaller, painted or transparent. Some Giselles even do without them, the wings merely suggested in the dance movements and the audience's mind. As for the sleeves, you may decide whether you want a little sleeve, as in *Les Sylphides,* or just a small fold of veil covering the area where the arm meets the shoulder.

The headdresses of course differ greatly, Giselle's headdress in particular having diminished over the decades. The old lithographs show us wreaths of flowers, worn like crowns. Grisi in Act II wore her wreath set back from the hairline, framing the face almost like a tiara. Today the *corps* may still wear wreaths, but Giselle usually settles for a small arrangement of flowers at either side of the head, or around the chignon. Of course a girl with very dark hair needs hardly anything—like Fracci, for example, with her white skin and black hair, the perfect ideal of the Romantic ballerina. A blond, on the other hand, has to fight for her life—or at least her hairline, which is apt to disappear under the lights if you're not careful.

But even here, small, subtle details can be introduced. Alonso and Fonteyn have both worn little round funeral wreaths—one over each ear, worked in with other details. I have a little St. Andrew's Cross, a *Croix de St. André,* in each of my little wreaths, set in very discreetly with other small, shining things.

Even the quality of the dancing shoes changes from one act to the next. The rule of thumb is: harder shoes for the first act, softer ones—completely smashed if possible—for the second.

It is almost a truism to state, once again, that Act II is about the dance and about fulfillment—or perhaps, the lack of it. In the passage that so moved Théophile Gautier, Heine describes the wilis' *Tanzlust*—literally translated, the love of dancing. But it can also mean desire, pleasure, almost lust; an unstilled, unappeasable hunger to complete the uncompleted. "The wilis," he wrote, "are betrothed girls who have died before their wedding day."

> *The poor young creatures cannot lie still in their graves. In their dead hearts, in their dead feet, there lingers yet the Tanzlust that they could never satisfy in life, and at midnight they rise up, assemble like a troop on the high road and woe unto the young man who may encounter them there! He must dance with them; they twine their arms around him with an unbridled frenzy, and he must dance without pause until he drops dead. Decked out in their wedding finery, their heads bedecked with flowers and fluttering ribbons, sparkling rings on their fingers, the Wilis dance, elf-like, in the moonlight. Their features, though snow-white, have a youthful beauty; they laugh with such fearsome merriment, such wanton amiability, so beckoningly; these dead bacchantes are irresistible.*

Through the joint efforts, therefore, of *Giselle*'s creators, the wilis became not only women after death, but also *dancers* after death.

The human imagination, having nothing else to go on, can conceive life after death only as it has known life this side of the grave. The betrothed woman, dead before her wedding, seeks fulfillment — or so the imagination would have it. Similarly the dancer-woman, killed before total achievement, still seeks fulfillment — through the dance, one that is now transformed and distilled, dancing her way with superhuman power into the absolute, becoming herself pure dance.

The man who does not know this and thus does not respect it, the ignorant who ventures onto hallowed ground, is therefore condemned — not by the dancers but by his own ignorance. In their madness they will kill him, scarcely aware that they have killed, even as they trample their victim underfoot, their one desire, to accomplish the ritual, to consummate in death what has been left uncompleted in life.

The wilis, therefore, are almost like sacrificial priestesses, their victims, the uninitiated who by their very presence desecrate the ritual and must pay the price—an ancient folk tradition and if you wished, you could probably draw a thin parallel between the punishment of Hilarion and that of King Pentheus in the Greek legend of the Bacchae.

These dead bacchantes are irresistible.

This makes the wilis far more than your regulation *corps de ballet,* more than a choreographic backdrop for the stars. They are an essential part of the drama, at once passive and active, implacable executioners and lifeless automatons. There's a sense almost of coagulation into death, the corpse-like cadaver quality that we associate in life with certain great emotional disorders, something of the catatonic feeling of the Mad Scene of the first act. In the second act, these things combine to create the robot-like action, the regimentation that makes the wilis totally subordinate to the Queen.

The Queen of the Wilis is of course the great conductor; she's the *chef d'orchestre* and she makes them dance wildly—they lose themselves in the madness of the dance, thoroughly conditioned, regimented creatures that they are. You know that they will have no memory of the murder, that they will remember only the frenzy of their dancing. There is no lingering exultation at the death of Hilarion, no personal feeling of pleasure or even vengefulness. They scatter as though nothing had happened, the rites accomplished, the victim already forgotten.

(*A propros* regimentation: The complete score of *Giselle* originally included a fugue for the wilis, much admired in its day, but also possibly a humorous comment on the discipline and regimentation of the *corps de ballet,* who would have to have a fugue *de rigueur,* a drilling of the wilis, so to speak, like a regiment from another world.)

But Giselle is only a newly baptized wili. Barely initiated, she is not even present at Hilarion's destruction; now suddenly Albrecht reappears and her sisters are about to destroy him—all of this in close succession. Yet her love, that one link with life, is still strong enough to turn her toward Albrecht and away from his executioners. You might even call her a non-integrated wili, not yet fully obedient, floating in a kind of limbo between life and death, trailing the traces of earthly ties that are as yet only freshly severed.

She approaches the Queen. Instead of submitting, she begs. Destruction having been brought upon her, she now tries in turn to prevent destruction, to preserve and continue her love, which is all that is left to her. Giselle knows that as long as she loves, she is alive, that those we love keep us alive—"Let him live…to remember me"—and that love is the only antidote to death and destruction.

It was here that I felt Ulanova rose to the heights of her greatness, departing from tradition, but in a way that had its own validity. I'll never forget her, standing before Albrecht at the gravesite, protecting him, arms extended in a manner almost more reminiscent of the Swan Queen. In that moment, she became as imperiously strong and commanding as Myrtha herself. It was as though Giselle had reached the height of power and command in direct competition with the Queen of the Wilis, not at all submissive, but bringing the implied battle of the wills completely to the fore. I had never seen a Giselle do that, but it worked. She was doing it with her own truth, her own conviction.

I remember, too, the near-ritualistic gestures in the adagio—the lifts, an addressing of oneself, as if in prayer, to the sky; the *penché arabesque*, a bowing to mother earth, both movements endowed with an almost liturgical quality.

Ulanova gave that second act a kind of grandeur—heroic yet lyric—but co-existing with that heroism was a heart-rending sincerity, impulsive and vulnerable. You really felt she was going through

75

it for the first time and indeed there were times when it seemed to me that I could actually hear words. This particular kind of eloquence I find shared by other Soviet dancers—not only because they must project on a bigger stage, but because of a certain conviction in their portrayal which is probably part of their training.

(The Russian lifts, of course, are just incredible, emphasizing the other-worldly quality of the second act—Giselle as a creature of the air, seemingly hovering above the man, who looks up in adoration. Once, while preparing *Giselle* at Jacob's Pillow, My Albrecht, Ivan Nagy—now of Ballet Theatre but Hungarian and Soviet trained— asked me about trying the Soviet version for Act II. Certainly, I said, being hardly likely to deprive myself of the luxury of a marvelously ready partner with those big Soviet lifts. And we did. And it was wonderful!)

While we are on the subject of the *pas de deux*, I must say something about the music and indeed the entire score.

Because of my work with Balanchine—and that includes dancing to just about every kind of music: Bach, Vivaldi, Tchaikovsky, Fauré, Stravinsky, Webern—I find I can no more consider a ballet in technical terms alone than I could in musical terms alone. To the Balanchine, or semi-Balanchine dancer, as I consider myself, picking up on the working aspect of the music is simply second nature— you must go all the way into the score—and I was never so pleased as when one critic commented that my Giselle was fully realized in musical terms.

To those who call the *Giselle* score corny, therefore, I reply: not at all. It is wonderful ballet music, perfect for every element of the drama and the choreography. This, it seems to me, cannot be stressed too much in any serious study of *Giselle*.

Sometimes I feel that the very accessibility of the *Giselle* score, its success as a theater piece, draws attention away from what Adam has actually accomplished as a composer: his unobtrusive but effective use of *leitmotifs*, the viola and violin, or cello and viola representing the intertwining voices of Giselle and Albrecht; the nervous orchestral mutterings that accompany Hilarion's movements; the dramatic passage launching Berthe's warning of the wilis, with its foreshadowing of Tchaikovsky's *Francesca da Rimini*; and of course the evocative music of the Act II *pas de deux*, which to my thinking can easily bear comparison with the Act II adagio from *Swan Lake*. (If you're interested, just listen first to the reprise of the *pas de deux* for Siegfried and Odette, then a comparable passage from the Adam work—Albrecht leaving the cross to join Giselle in the great adagio—the pairing of lovers matched in each case by a similar pairing in the score: two orchestral voices joined in major sixths, a musical representation of the two yearning to be one.)

I have not dwelled on the specific events in this act because it does not seem to me to be necessary. Act II, for all its drama, is essentially a drama of the mind and the spirit, acted out on a higher, more abstracted plane than that of the costumed story ballet of Act I. But to conclude:

The dancing increases in intensity, reaching its climax just as morning intervenes. The wilis disperse. Giselle must return to the grave. Albrecht, driven to the brink of death, has been spared, matured by his ordeal.

Seen in this light, Bathilde's re-appearance—included in the original production, now no longer in use—must have had a certain validity: the princess as the call of duty, accepted by a man now ready to assume his station in life, with all its responsibilities.

Today's productions dispense with the Princess, emphasizing rather a last glimpse of the lovers together—i.e., leave those two alone—then Albrecht on the empty stage, facing the future and a new reality. Both endings, however, are germane to the same point—that this has become Albrecht's story as well as Giselle's, their two destinies linked by the power of her love. The thoughtless boy of the first act has become the tragic hero of the second. Though ready to die, he has been given a second chance. He has seen the possibility of his own destruction and emerged with a new awareness — that he has been *allowed* to continue, that life is a gift, that love in turn gives life and that the force of love has been his salvation.

He has been given back to life; he has been given the gift of understanding.

Giselle on the Road
Some Notes on Production

Not so long ago, the great classics were pretty much the property of the large, internationally known companies. Today, thanks to a thriving regional ballet movement, they are being staged by resident companies all over America. I myself have danced Giselle with a number of good local troupes and would therefore like to close with a few notes on staging, and the particular concerns of a soloist.

On coming to a town, I always begin by checking out the stage on which I'm going to dance; that is my first consideration. Is it hard? Is it slippery? Is it smooth? Is it dangerous? In other words, what kind of surface will I have to deal with—because the harder the surface, the softer the shoes. Then there's the matter of the lighting and the decor. I always, for example, check the door of Giselle's cottage—is it in working order, does it open in or out? (I remember a friend of mine, guesting with a European company, who was not informed about the door, couldn't get it open, and missed her entrance. The orchestra played Giselle's entrance, but all the audience saw was a shaking cottage as she struggled, unseen, with the doorknob; it was what dancers have nightmares about.)

No, you must check the doors, the props, the distances, the bench—is it in the right place? If the stage is very small it must be placed out of the way so that you can jump about without any trouble. In short, it's like the situation of an actor looking after accessories—they must be accounted for, they must look familiar, they must be integrated into your performance, just as your performance must be integrated with that of the other dancers.

The local company of course knows their resources better than I as guest artist. They usually prepare their own *corps de ballet.* But we get together on matters relating to my role, and if I feel that some suggestions on my part may help, I offer them. Company conditions of course vary. The mime tradition, for example —generally stronger in Europe than in the United States—is still being built up among the newer companies and you may find yourself working with a Berthe played by the youngest dancer in the troupe, who may in turn need help with her makeup and her mime passages. I often think it would be useful to have a set of guidelines, to be adjusted according to the resources of the individual companies— a written indication, perhaps, of the various dialogues in their essential points: the Mother with Giselle, the Mother with the peasants, Bathilde and Giselle, Bathilde with her father, Bathilde with Albrecht. The company could then decide how much they wished to retain.

By now I know the other roles quite well; in fact I cheerfully admit to being one Giselle who's always wanted to play Hilarion. Anyway, there's usually some meeting of the minds on Giselle's relationship to the other protagonists. We talk, we try things out. My own tendency is to suggest adding material—to lengthen the story a bit, add a little more meat if possible. If I come with an Albrecht, that relationship has been worked out ahead of time. But if I dance with the company Albrecht, I generally like to work with him a good deal. The object, again, is to achieve an integrated effect—not of someone who has flown into town two days before, but a Giselle who looks as if she had been literally born there.

Finally, there's the music; taped in some cases, full orchestra in others. If there's to be an orchestra, I will send the conductor a tape—a recording indicating the sort of tempi we will want for the sections we'll be dancing. The resident company of course decides on what is right for their own dancers. In absolute luxury conditions I would want to work a little with the instrumental soloists—with the viola, the violin, the cello; if there's a good harp, so much the better.

Thanks to LP's we now know what the uncut *Giselle* score sounds like; not that it's absolutely essential to have all those cuts re-opened, but it does offer at least the possibility, should one wish it, of reviving certain aspects of the original production. A choreographer may want to interpolate additional sections—a little more dancing for the corps or perhaps an extra bit of pantomime, using local resources to do it. Conversely, if he or she feels that the company cannot sustain too great a degree of exposure and wants to do something in good taste, some good cuts may suggest themselves, leaving everybody satisfied.

Violette Verdy

In the summer of 1976, after an 18-year stay with the New York City Ballet, Violette Verdy accepted an appointment as Directrice de la Danse at the Paris Opéra. Thus her career has come full circle, for it was with the Paris Opéra Ballet that Miss Verdy, for a short time, trained as a child, one of the thirty or so children who were chosen to be *les petit rats* of the Opéra Ballet just after the close of the Second World War. Quite soon thereafter, at the age of 11, Miss Verdy made her Paris debut, dancing in *Les Forains* with Roland Petit's Ballet des Champs-Elysées.

Since that time, Miss Verdy has been performing to critical and popular acclaim with companies in Europe and America, as well as appearing on stage, television, and in film. She moved to New York City in 1957 and danced with the American Ballet Theatre for one year, after which George Balanchine and Lincoln Kirstein invited her to join with the New York City Ballet. She became a principal dancer with that company, delighting audiences with her distinctive flair for nuance within Balanchine's disciplined choreography, and Balanchine created many leading roles for her in such ballets as *Tchaikovsky Pas de deux, Jewels,* and *A Midsummer Night's Dream.* Miss Verdy received the Dance Magazine Award in 1967, and in 1971 the French government presented her with the Chevalier de l'Ordre des Arts et Lettres.

Ann Sperber

This is not the first time that Ann Sperber has used her writing and publishing talents in the field of the performing arts. As senior editor for G. P. Putnam's Sons and McGraw-Hill Book Company, she produced a number of prize-winning books related to opera, and her writings have appeared in such publications as *The New York Times Book Review*, *Opera News*, and *The American Record Guide*. She has written extensively on the Dance Collection of the New York Public Library at Lincoln Center and on the Jerome Robbins Archive of dance film, belonging to the Collection.

Born in Vienna and raised in New York City, Ann Sperber attended the High School of Music and Art, the Juilliard School of Music, and Barnard College, after which she studied at the University of West Berlin as a Fulbright Fellow. She is a member of the Executive Council of the New York City Opera Guild.

Marcia Brown

In her rural Connecticut home not far from New York City, Marcia Brown works in the various media—painting, drawing, woodcut, and photography, to name just a few—that have marked her distinguished artistic career. Children's books created by her have twice won the Caldecott Medal, as well as the Regina Medal, and have been exhibited by the New York Society of Illustrators. Her prints have been shown at the New School for Social Research, the Carnegie Institute, the Brooklyn Museum, and several galleries.

In her early adolescence, already occupied with drawing, writing, and music, Marcia Brown acquired a passion for the dance. *Giselle* is one of her favorite of all ballets, and she has seen almost a hundred performances of it by most of the major ballet companies of our time. The drawings in this book are the result of countless sketches at rehearsals and performances as she studied the dancers' movements, the decor and costumes, the music, and the choreography.